My BIG BOOK of Bible Stories

VOLUME TWO

In him was life, and that life was the light of men.
John 1:4 NIV

The Creation Story 2

Adam and Eve 18

Cain and Abel 34

David and Goliath..48

© 2011 by Phil A. Smouse
ISBN 9781726798266

All rights reserved. No part of this publication may be reproduced or transmitted for commercial purposes, except for brief quotations in printed reviews, without written permission of the author.

All scripture quotations, unless otherwise indicated, are taken from the New King James Version®. Copyright © 1982 by Thomas Nelson, Inc. Used by permission. All rights reserved. Scripture quotations marked NIV are taken from the Holy Bible, New International Version®. NIV®Copyright © 1973, 1978, 1984 by International Bible Society. Used by permission.

In the beginning, way back at its birth,
God created the heavens and cooked up the earth.
Without a big-bang or a pop or a fizz—
out of *nothing at all*—He made all that there is!

The earth was asleep in the darkness of night—
until God told the darkness, "Now let there be light!"
And light was! And that very first blazing, clear light
was the light of His glory, His love, and His might.

God looked at the light. He saw it was good.
It was lighting things up just the way that it should.
His love rolled up the darkness and chased it away. . .

There was evening and morning, the very first day.

Then God said, "Let the waters that cover the world
be untangled, uncorked, opened up and unfurled.
Let them gather above. Let them billow and puff
into cloudy-white, pillowy cotton and fluff.

Let them gather below—let them bubble and splash—
let them babble and gurgle and splatter and crash!

Let the sky stay up high. Let the sea stay down low."
And that's just what they did, as you probably know.
And as *you* may have guessed—and as I now know, too. . .

There was evening and morning on day number two.

Oh, but day number three—it was something to see—
it was something to see back on day number three!
For on day number three God said, *"Now* let there be
lumpy clods of dry sod where there used to be sea!"

And so up from the gurgling, bubbling deep—
up and up from their slumbery, salty, blue sleep,
there arose mighty mountains of muddy, brown goop—
sopping, soggy, wet piles of primordial soup!

God called that goop "land" and the rest he called "sea,"
and He dried it all up just for you and for me.
Then He said, "Let My land produce veggies and fruits,
from their stems and their shoots all the way to their roots!"

So that's just what they did. It was something to see,
on that morning and evening of day number three.

You say your head's spinning? Well, mine's spinning, too.
With all that God's done, what more could He do?
Oh but then, once again, as the night softly spread,
God unfolded the silence and silently said,

"Now let there be lights in the darkness of space—
tiny, twinkling star-lights all over the place—
glassy, golden-light, spinning-white, sparkling spheres.

Let them sing out the seasons and mark out the years!"

And the sun came alive with the gift of His light,
and it shone with the light of His love and His life!
And then high in the inky-blue black of the night
He ker-plopped down the moon to reflect back its light.

What a day? *I should say!* Could there be any more,
after morning and evening on day number four?

But on day number five the whole world came alive—
came alive and went right into wild overdrive!

"Let the waters be filled up with whales and with fish,
and all manner of things that swim, swiggle, and swish.
And then," said the Lord, "let each salmon and tuna
in every last lake, river, sea, and lagoona—

Each grunion and grunt, every grouper and crappie—
each wahoo and halibut mammy and pappy
live happily, *snappily*, every last one
with a million fish daughters and little fish sons!

Let the skies fill with twittering, chirping, and tweeting,
with cock-a-doo doodling, honking, and peeping—
with chickadees, hummingbirds, roosters, and hens—
tufted titmouses, red robins, and wrens!

God saw all the dancing and splashing and singing,
the laughter and joy that His love had been bringing.
He saw it was good. It was free and alive!

There was morning and evening on day number five.

Then on day number six God pulled ALL the stops.
Of all days—some say—that *this day* was tops!
For when *this day* was through, all that God had begun—
all the work that He worked—would at last be all done.

"Let the land dart and scurry with fuzzy and furry things—
wild and wonderful, cuddly and purry things!
Lions and tigers and zebras and yaks,
topped with horns and antennas—with antlers and racks.

Hairy things. *Scary things!* Up-all-nightmarey things!
Cute little, snuggle-me-soft, teddy-beary things.
Doo-dads and whatzits and thingamajigs.
Porcupines—prairie dogs—pot-bellied pigs!

Let them toddle and flip. Let them slither and sprawl.
Let the land creep and crawl with new life, big and small!"

God looked all around and He saw it was good.
Every thing did its thing just the way that it should.
Every happy new heart sang His praise, loud and clear,
for they knew something BIG was about to appear.

"Now let Us make man—let Us make him alone—
in Our image and likeness," said God from His throne.
Let him love and be loved. Let him know and be known.
Let him rule Our creation and make it his home."

So in His own image God made up the man—
male and female He made them, just as He'd planned.
Without cavemen or monkeys or riddles or tricks. . .

There was evening and morning on day number six.

On day seven God rested from all He had done.
He had finished the work that His hands had begun.
And he took that one day, and He called that day blessed,
and He set it apart there from all of the rest.

So this Sunday, I think I know just what I'll do:
I'll plop down on my knees and say, "Thanks!"
Wouldn't you?

For each breath that we take—every beat of our hearts—
is a *gift,* and without Him we truly would not
have one slender, slim thing. *We'd have nothing.* It's true!

Oh the depth of His love! *I'll remember.* Will YOU?

By the sound of His voice, in the still of the night,
long before the first whisper of darkness or light,
on a wee-tiny, shiny, blue ball out in space
God began an amazing, mysterious place.

For with hands never heard, and with eyes never seen
God created a garden—silent and green—
then filled it with things that hum, bubble, and buzz—
full of all that there is, ever *would be,* or was!

But something was missing—some one or some *who*.
So God reached down in to the muck and the goo,
and there, with a handful of soggy, wet sod,
from a squishy-wet, wee, water-loggy, brown clod,

from the dust and the dirt—from the muck and the clay—
God created the very first man on that day!

And that man who God made from the dust and debris,
yes that made-out-of-muddy-brown-muck-man is ME!

And God breathed and said, "Adam"—and POW! I arose.
Then He washed off my hands and untangled my toes
and said, *"Pick up your clippers and haul out the hose—*
go take care of My garden and see that it grows!"

So I watered the lilies. I fluffed up the flowers.
I patted the bunnies for hours and hours.

But oh, I was lonely as lonely can be.
Not one bunny or bee was as lonely as me!
For as often I say, and as everyone knows,
every guy needs a girl everywhere that he goes.

So one night as I snuggled all soft in my bed—
as sweet visions and dreams danced around in my head—
God knelt down and He plucked-out a rib from my side. . .

And He made me my very own beautiful bride!

Well I looked at that girl and my heart went KER-THUMP!
My poor throat crimped and crinkled-up into a lump!
But I reached out my hand—*and she reached out hers, too!*
It was love at first how-do-you, *wow*-do-you do!

And right there in the night we embraced—and we kissed.
Then we both heard God's voice. . .

We both heard Him say this:

"I Am God. I Am One. I Am Faithful and True!
I made all of this stuff just for you and for you.
You may fill up your tummies with gladness and glee
with the yummy, good, fruit found on any old tree.

But whatever you hear, and whatever you do,
you must never—not ever—chomp, nibble, or chew
on the juicy, pink fruit of THIS tree—not at all.

If you eat from this tree, if you dare to, or try,
on the day that you do you will both surely die!"

So we did what God said. Yes, we did what we should,
because God was our God, and oh boy, was God good!
We'd both giggle and play every night and each day. . .

'til we met up with old you-know-who, as they say!

He thlid-down from that tree with a thlippery thlump,
then he curled up his rump in a leathery lump,
and he slithered right up to my sweet, little wife
and with four little words that snake ruined our life!

"Did God really say?" hissed that slobbery slug,
"You must never gulp, nibble, chomp, gobble, or glug
from the yummy, pink fruit found on every good tree
in my beautiful garden of Eden—*did He?"*

"It's a joke. It's a trick. It's a fib and a lie!
Go ahead—eat the fruit. *You will not surely die!"*

Eve looked at the fruit, and you know, it looked good!
And for one tiny second she thought that she could
just go right-on ahead and just do her own thing—

as if God wasn't there. As if God didn't care—
as if God wasn't God every day, everywhere!

So she did it! She ate it!
Then I ate it, too!

And the very next half-a-split-second we knew. . .

I looked up at Eve, and then Eve looked at me. . .
Then Eve started to *scream,* and I started to flee!
For I noticed her toe—then she noticed my knee.
So she jumped in a bush, and I ran up a tree!

And *right then and right there,* as we quivered and quaked,
we both knew we'd been tricked by that sneaky, old snake.

But we did what we did, and we *knew* we were wrong—
and we knew that God knew—so it wouldn't be long
'til we'd both have to face Him, and face Him we would.
And we knew He'd remove us from Eden for good.

And that's just what God did.
But we gave Him no choice.
Our hearts were both fooled
by that sneaky snake's voice!

The devil's a LIAR.
He always will be!

So whatever you hear, and whatever you do,
and *whatever* that snake tries to get you to do,
please remember God's love—and remember our sin.
There is only one God. Listen only to Him!

cain and abel

Genesis 4:1-16

A long time ago, in a faraway place,
near a garden that bloomed with God's love and His grace,
lived two men who were different as different could be—
Cain and Abel, the offspring of Adam and Eve.

Cain worked the soil. He dug and he hoed.
He burrowed and furrowed. He mulched and he mowed.
He weeded and feeded the seed he had sown,
'til his garden was monstrously, miracle-grown!

Oh, but Abel was different, for Abel liked sheep.

Yes, he loved them so much he saw sheep in his sleep.

And their baahs and their bleats didn't bug him a bit.

He loved every wooly, wee one he could get.

One day as he wandered and waggled and walked
through the grassy, green hills with his fluffy, white flock,
by the quiet, still water he paused and he stopped. . .
and he thought, *"Oh my goodness. I almost forgot!"*

"Our God is so good, and He's blessed me so much,
with my little, bo-sheepily people and such,
I should bring Him a present—a thank-ewe—a kid!
So that's just what I'll do." And that's just what he did.

But when Cain saw what Abel was able to do
with his tender, kind heart and his loving thank-ewe,
he looked *down* at the ground, and he grumbled and stewed,
and he thought, "I guess *I should give* God a gift, too."

So they both brought the very best gift that they could.
Abel gave his with joy. Cain just knew that he should.
And from way up in heaven, God looked *at their hearts*—
for He knew that *Cain's gift* was *no gift* from the start.

"Cain, why are you angry? Why grumble and stew,
when you KNOW," the LORD said, "what I want you to do?
When you do what is right, it's My joy and delight—
but the choice is one-hundred percent up to you."

But Cain would not listen. He just didn't care
about anyone, any-which-way, anywhere.
So he tuned out God's voice, and the minute he did,
sin was waiting to get him—*and get him it did!*

So he hatched up a plan right up there in his head—
a BIG, bug-eyed, nasty, red, rotten plan fed
by *the devil himself*—by his anger and gall—
to get rid of his brother *for once and for all!*

Cain knew what he did. It was there on his hands.
It was there *in his heart*—on the ground—in the sand.

And the ground cried aloud
for the thing Cain had done.

There was nowhere to go. There was nowhere to run.
There was nowhere to hide from the blazing, hot sun,
as the sound of God's voice, and each drop of red blood
thundered, *"Where is your brother, and what have you done!?"*

"I swear I don't know. God, you surely must see!
I would not have done THAT! It could not have been ME!"
Cain lied and he lied, and way, deep down inside
all the love he once had simply gave up and died.

For the rest of his life—to his very last day—
Cain just wandered and squandered his life clean away.
All his beautiful gardens dried up into dust,
in the very same way that they will, and they must,

when a heart grows so blind, and so callous and cold—
so angry and bitter—so crinkled and old—
that it won't even notice the glittering gold,
of the true heart of Jesus in every last soul.

"BIGGER is better. Yes, bigger is *best*.
When you're BIGGER you're better than all of the rest.
For as everyone knows, and can gladly recall,
when you're dinky and small you don't matter at all!"

Is THAT what you're thinking? Is that what you said?
Is that what's been running around in your head?

Well, just settle-on-down in your chair or your bed
with your mom or your dad or your great-uncle Ted
and I think, if you listen, you're going to see
that BIG isn't all that it's cracked up to be!

Bigger is BETTER!

Two armies were gathered on two distant hills.
But the army on one gave the other the chills!
Both armies were fuming and ready to fight,
and it looked like at any time now they just might—

when what to their wondering eyes did appear,
but a creature so terrible, mean, and severe
that each man in *God's* army—each soldier and spear—
was french-frazzled with fear from the front to the rear!

He was biggeth and talleth and largeth and higheth.
He stretched from the ground straight up to the sky-eth!
Armed to the teeth both above and beneath;
a big, burly, Philistine *giant*—

Goliath!

But *this* was no jolly-green "ho-ho-ho" boy.
No, THIS was a NINE-FOOT-TALL search-and-destroy-boy—
a steaming mad, armor-clad, Oscar-the-Grouch,
with a burning desire to make you say, *"Ouch!"*

"YOO-HOO? Boys!" Goliath spat.
"Come out and play—I brought my bat!
You say you're all fuming and ready to fight?
Then *put up your dukes!* Have at it—all right?"

So they put up their dukes—every one, one and all—
but their dukes were all saggy and baggy and small,
and they knew if they made just one pip or wee-squeak,
he would round them and pound them clean into next week!

"Okay, I'm a reasonable, sensitive guy,
and I see," said Goliath, "you're ready to cry.
So I'll make you a deal. Yes, here's just what I'll do.
Here's a special one-time-only offer for you:

I'll fight for *my* army—just little old me—
against one of *your* men. So then, who will it be?
Yes, that will be lovely! Oh, that *will* be fun,
and there won't be a mess to clean up when we're done!"

"Come on, what's the matter?" he bellowed and thundered.
"Please step right on up and get clobbered and plundered!
Don't want to get dirty? Still frozen with fright?
Well then maybe your MOMMIES will come out and fight!"

So, night after night after day after day,
on and on went Goliath that very same way.
And for forty long days, on their side of the hill,
they just stood there like statues, and took it, until. . .

A wee-tiny fellow, so dinky and small
that you'd hardly believe he would matter at all,
wandered into the camp and just happened to hear
all the, *"fee-fie-foe-fum!"* that had filled them with fear.

"Just who does this Philistine think that he is?"
said that dinky, small dude with that big voice of his.
"He's insulting the army of Almighty God!
but he'll do it *no more,* over my own wee-bod!"

Well now, THAT kind of talk turned some heads right away.
No, that's not like the thing that you hear every day!

So when word got around, that wee-dinky, small dude
was shipped off to the king, who was coming unglued.
Yes, the king was *upset*. And why shouldn't he be?
He had to whip someone as big as a TREE!

ACME
SECRET
WEAPON A

SHIP TO
KING
SAUL

Oh, but when he saw David, his tummy flip-flopped.
His heart sunk down to his sandals and stopped.
They needed a hero—a fighting *machine*.
But Dave looked like HE couldn't whip a sardine!

"This kid is a tadpole! A pee-wee! A guppy!
We need a HE-MAN," said the king, "not a *puppy*.
Now, pardon me, son. You're a cute little tike,
but we need a KING KONG not a boy on a bike!"

"My name, sir, is *David*, and if I may say,"
said that wee-tiny guy in his extra-large way,
"that I've beat-up a bear and I've clobbered a lion,
and whipped them both *good*, sir—without even tryin'!

For GOD is my strength, and although I'm quite small,
by His might and His power *Goliath will fall!*
You say you need someone who's manly and tough?
Then come over here king, and I'll show you my stuff!"

"Well, aren't *you* a spunky, young, Godly, good guy!
All right," said the king, "let's go give it a try."

So the king gave wee David his helmet and boots,
and his shield and his sword and his giant-proof suit,
and he figured that David was ready to fight,
when in fact he was locked-down and frozen-up tight!

"I CAN'T fight like this! Man, I can't even see!
This might work for YOU, but it won't work for ME.
I said this before, but I'll say it again:
It's GOD who will fight, and it's GOD who will win!"

So David de-booted, disrobed. and undressed.
He untangled that old tin-can-tankerous mess,
bolted down to the stream, gathered five smooth, small stones,
then took off like the wind, bent to rattle some bones!

"Hey, giant!" Dave yelled.
"Yeah, I'm talking to YOU!
Hey, I'm telling you just what I'm going to do!
You've insulted the army of Almighty God—
Now you better get ready to swallow some sod!"

Well, Goliath looked down just below his left knee,
oh, and what, to his wondering eyes, did he see
but a wee-teeny fellow, so dinky and small
that you'd hardly believe he could matter at all!

"What am I, A DOG?!?" thundered mean old Goliath,
"that you send me this wee-teeny, not-very-higheth,
pink, peach-fuzzy pup with a stick and some rocks?
Oooh, I'm shakin' the whole way on down to my socks."

"Well then fight like a man!" rumbled dinky, small Dave.
"What's the matter, you sissy? Come on—*make my day!*
This battle is GOD'S, and in GOD'S mighty name,
on this day *I'M the hunter* and YOU are the GAME!"

And so out came his sling, and then in went a stone,
and wee, dinky, small Dave, in a way all his own,
slung it 'round and around and around and about,
and that one-tiny, smooth-shiny pebble flew out. . .

like a photon-torpedo—like *lightning* it sped—
and it bopped old Goliath right-square in the head!

"My word!" said Goliath, "You ARE a good shot!
I was going to duck, but I guess I forgot.
Why is everyone spinning? Who turned out the lights?
Is it nap time already? Oh well, nighty-night!"

And right there in that spot,
in the blink of an eye,
that gigantic, enormous,
big muscle-bound guy
went as soft as a Twinkie—
he pitched and he yawed. . .

And fell down with a

CRASH!

fat-head-first in the sod.

You can puff yourself up. It won't help you at all.

For the bigger you are, then the harder you'll fall.

But when GOD is your strength, you're a hundred feet tall. . .

Even though you're the smallest, wee person of all.

write to Phil A. Smouse

Once upon a time, Phil A. Smouse wanted to be a scientist.

But scientists don't get wonderful letters and pictures from friends like you. So Phil decided to draw and color instead! He and his wife live in Lancaster Pennsylvania. They have two children they love with all their heart.

Phil loves to tell kids like you all about Jesus. He would love to hear from you today! So get out your markers and crayons and send a letter or a picture to:

phil@philsmouse.com

Or visit his website at http://www.philsmouse.com/

Made in the USA
Monee, IL
11 February 2020